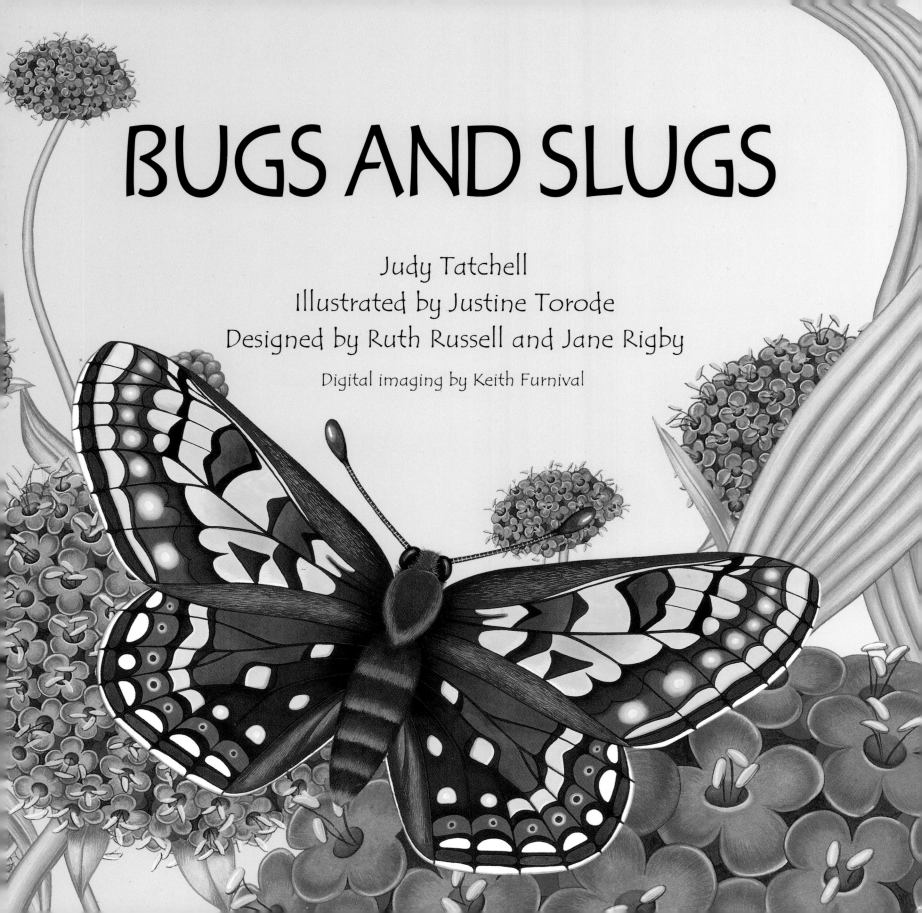

BUGS AND SLUGS

Judy Tatchell

Illustrated by Justine Torode

Designed by Ruth Russell and Jane Rigby

Digital imaging by Keith Furnival

Bees and wasps

Can you find a bee on this page? It's collecting a sweet liquid called nectar from a flower.

Bee

Wasps love sweet things. They are a nuisance if they come after your food.

Wasp

If a wasp or bee is scared, it might sting, so don't try to hit it.

This is a bumble bee. It is looking for nectar.

Is that a bee or a wasp on the peach? Lift the flap to see.

Spiders

Spiders eat flies and other insects. They make sticky webs to catch them.

A spider makes a new web each morning.

Spiders have oily feet. These stop them from getting stuck in their webs.

This fly has just flown into the web.

Worms

Worms break up soil as they burrow. This helps plants push their roots into the soil.

It isn't easy to tell which end of a worm is the front!

A worm moves by stretching out the front of its body.

Front of worm

Back of worm

Then it pulls the back part forward.

Butterflies

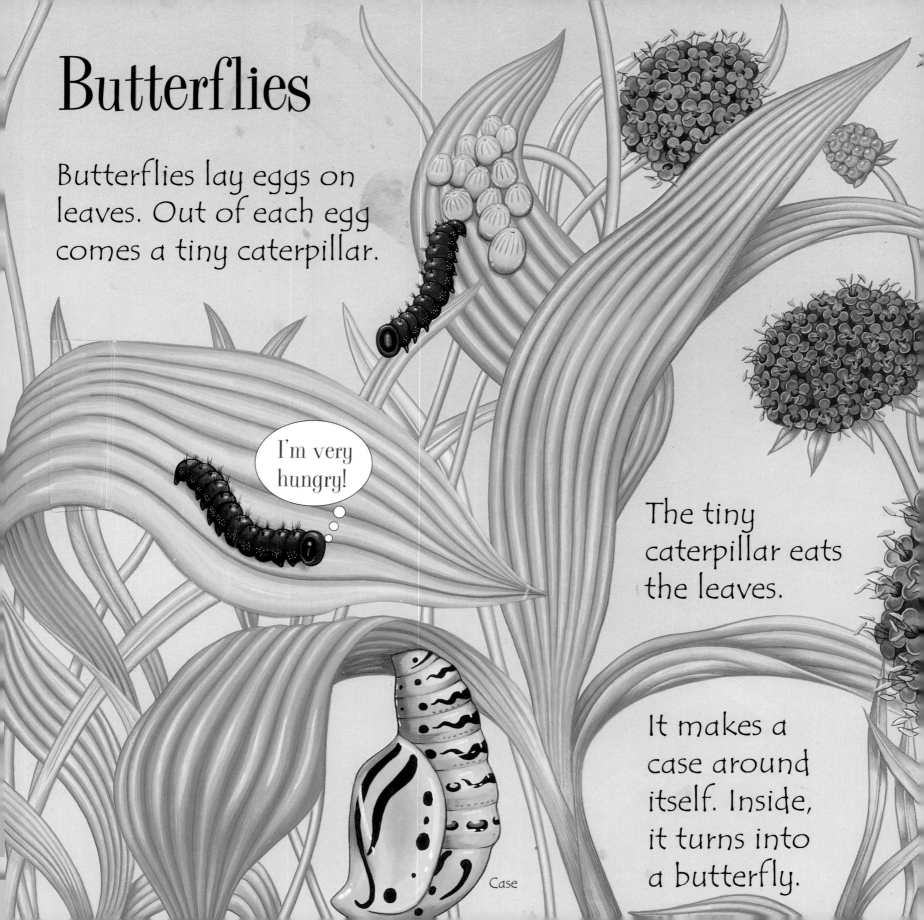

Butterflies lay eggs on leaves. Out of each egg comes a tiny caterpillar.

I'm very hungry!

The tiny caterpillar eats the leaves.

It makes a case around itself. Inside, it turns into a butterfly.

Case

After a few weeks, the butterfly comes out of its case.

It stretches its wings and flies away.

Flies

Flies taste through their feet. They walk on things to find out if they want to eat them.

It's very hard to swat flies because they whizz around so fast.

If a fly with dirty feet walks on your food, the dirt might make you ill.

If you see a fly near food...

Ladybirds and greenflies

Ladybirds are easy to see. You can count their spots.

Ladybirds like to eat greenflies. Can you see a ladybird having a snack?

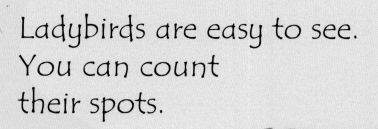

If the ladybird eats all the greenflies...

Greenflies suck a liquid, called sap, from buds. The buds dry up. A dry bud won't open into a flower.

Slugs and snails

Slugs and snails like damp, cool places.

What's eating this lettuce?

Munch Munch

Snails can't see well, but they are good at smelling and feeling.

I'm safe in here!

Some birds eat snails. They have to break the shell.

Who's at the end of this shiny trail?

If snails and slugs dry out, they can't make slime.

A snail's shell helps stop it from drying out in the sun.

Beetles

Beetles like to live among leaves and sticks. They eat tiny insects.

Wing case

A beetle has two hard, shiny wing cases over its wings. These keep its wings safe.

Wing case

When a beetle flies, it holds its wing cases out of the way.

Centipedes and millipedes

A centipede is very wriggly. It eats smaller creatures. It has to run quickly to catch its food.

Centipede

A millipede eats plants. It has more legs than a centipede but it can't run as quickly!

Millipede

Whose tail is this?

This book has shown you just some of the tiny creatures that you can find living in your garden. Why not explore for yourself to see how many more you can discover there?

Buzzzzzzzzzzzz

Edited by Sarah Khan

This new, enlarged edition first published in 2004 by Usborne Publishing Ltd,
Usborne House, 83-85 Saffron Hill, London EC1N 8RT, England.
www.usborne.com
Copyright © Usborne Publishing Ltd, 2004, 1999.

Printed in China.

zzzzzzzzzzzzzzzzzzzzzzzzzzzzZZZZZZZZZZZZZZZ